My name ____________

My phone # ____________

My cello teacher ____________

Kaleidoscopes

for cello

Book 1

a child-centered, Kodály-inspired
approach to cello study by

Elise Winters

ISBN 978-1-959675-08-2

About the Author

Elise Winters began her music studies at the age of four in the cradle of the Suzuki community in Frederick, Maryland. She continued with internationally renowned Suzuki teacher Ronda Cole and with Elisabeth Adkins, associate concertmaster of the National Symphony Orchestra. A graduate *summa cum laude* of Rice University in English and Music and a University of Texas Presidential Scholar with a Master of Social Work, she has performed with the Austin Symphony Orchestra for more than two decades and is a widely admired chamber musician and soloist.

Elise has extensive training in both Suzuki and Kodály methodologies. Her interests extend to developmental psychology, linguistics, cognition, communication, biomechanics, and ecstatic dance. Her diverse background has placed her in a unique position to write an inter-disciplinary, child-focused cello method.

Elise resides in Austin, Texas. Whenever she is not teaching or performing, she can be found enjoying Indian curry, sipping a latte at Monkey Nest Coffee, or dancing.

This book is dedicated to the memory of Paul Schratz, a navy officer by career and violinist by love. Growing up just 60 miles away from her birth family, Elise never met her birth grandfather, but his love for music lives on in her work.

About the Illustrator

Originally from a small seaside town in New Jersey, Tony Sansevero runs Magical Ideas Illustration, an art studio in Austin Texas. His projects include books, murals, private commissions, and a whimsically Gothic haunted house installation recognized as one of Austin's neighborhood gems. Although he works in a variety of illustration styles, he specializes in children's art. He has illustrated over 20 books including the award-winning "Sixth Grade Aliens" series by Bruce Coville, which was adapted into a popular television show.

Table of Contents

Front Matter

Repertoire

Skills & Checklists

Note to the Teacher

The Kaleidoscopes approach takes the best aspects of Suzuki, Montessori, and Kodaly and synthesizes them into a comprehensive, child-centered method for instrumental learning.

Comments on the First Edition. This edition of Kaleidoscopes Book 1 for Cello is being released in its early stages so that it can be available for teachers and families to enjoy sooner rather than later. The book has not yet gone through the same multi-year review process as the corresponding violin books.

Cello teachers are invited to observe their students' progress through the book and write the author with any and all suggestions regarding the Movement Building Blocks (which are designed to prepare and reinforce posture concepts), song ordering, sequencing of technical concepts, and individual song teaching points.

Two important components will be added for young cellists in the coming several years: 1) Several songs which were added specifically for the cello books (and did not exist in the violin books) are still awaiting vocal recordings; and 2) The companion parent guide for cello, *The Balanced Cellist*, will need to be created. The completion of these elements will be a multi-year process.

For the present moment, teachers may use articles from *The Balanced Violinist* to provide parent education and as a reference for the bowing patterns and exercises at the back of this book.

Establishing the Left Hand Shape. The first two songs (*Quaker, Quaker and Pease Porridge*) are *so-mi-do* songs and can be played in any position. If played in first position, the open string and 3rd finger would be used. The hand shape is set from the perpendicular angle of the 3rd finger.

As a suggested alternative, particularly for younger players, playing these songs in third position offers the benefit of establishing the posture without the common problems of the student twisting, craning, or moving the cello further away in order to see their fingers. If played in third position, it is the 4th finger which sets the hand. The finger spacing in this position is more comfortable than first position, which will generally improve intonation.

Third rather than fourth position is chosen because 1) The thumb can be located in its ideal location across from 2nd finger; 2) The strings are easier to press; and 3) The bow lane is more similar to first position, and is easier to reach.*

A third song, *Fireflies*, is designed to be played in third position using only fingers 1, 3, and 4.

When the teacher is ready to introduce first position (in preparation for Hot Cross Buns), the first three measures of *Old Joe Clark* offer a fun transition activity. The descending scale is played as a "one-finger scale," mapping the intermediate positions. If desired, an additional measure can be added, modified with a note doubling to avoid crossing to the lower string.

Bow Usage. The first nine songs – through *All Around the Buttercup* – are played near the balance point. These establish the whole-arm movement and the use of the shoulder as a hinge.

The first learning of the third piece, *Fireflies*, should be at the balance point; however, its soft and delicate nature offers an opportunity to introduce bowing above the middle (hinging at the elbow) in preparation for full-bow playing. This should be a later upgrade, once the student is further along.

Mary Had a Little Lamb, Twinkle, Hush-a-Bye, The Koi, and similar songs offer opportunities for legato and fuller bows when the student is ready. *The Koi* is a new arrangement of the familiar *French Folk Song* from Suzuki, allowing this beloved song to shine with more child-friendly lyrics than its 18th century source material, which modern listeners would find bizarre.

Key Sequence & Left Hand Development. *Hot Cross Buns* and subsequent songs can be introduced in G major for ease of bowing, or in D major for greater ease of the left hand – whichever best facilitates students' setup and comfort.

After the first few songs, the student should be able to settle into D major as their "home key." Approximately a dozen short songs are played in this key, with the use of fourth finger and string crossings being gradually increased during this period.

* Fourth position was initially planned for young students, and the repertoire recording was made before this was revised. For this reason, the video shows fourth position for *Quaker, Quaker* and *Pease Porridge*. The audio recording has been adjusted down one whole step.

Once the student is playing fluently in D major, the same dozen songs will be moved to C major, with 4th finger tonic. The transposition activity makes it clear to students early in their study why 3rd finger must be used at some times, and 2nd finger at others – it is not a random "fact" about a given piece of music, but rather is a result of where the *mi-fa* half-step falls in a given key.

Once the new key of C major has been mapped onto familiar songs, literature which uses the lower leading tone (i.e. low *ti*) can now be introduced. These songs will use both 2nd finger (*fa*) and 3rd finger (*ti*). They include familiar favorites such as *Yankee Doodle* and *Bingo*, as well as the beloved German folk song *The Birds' Wedding*.

Transposition will be used throughout students' Kaleidoscopes journey to help them "map" familiar melodies and tonal patterns (e.g. the tonic arpeggio, low and high *do*, the lower leading tone, etc.) into new keys. The language of solfège allows the patterns to be more easily observed, recognized, and remembered.

Bowings. A majority of the bowings printed in this book are considered optional at the Book 1 level; students are free to focus the majority of their attention on posture and technique during this time. The bowings offered in the notation provide an optional upgrade, to be introduced by the teacher for the student who is ready to add this element.

On a related note, many of the rhythms have been slightly altered from the vocal version of the song, to provide better playability as well as to simplify the irregularities of the text. Wherever this is the case, either version may be played, according to whatever is easiest and most intuitive and for the student.

Extensions. The lower leading tone, "low *ti*," is a frequent and important tonal feature, but comes with a physical challenge for the novice cellist. For this reason, the need to introduce this note (and skill) is delayed through the addition of Mixolydian, Aeolian, and Dorian songs (*Old Joe Clark*, *Shady Grove*, and *Crabfish*, respectively) which use a lowered 7th scale degree.

Backward extensions are introduced toward the end of Book 1 using review material (see the checklist at the back). Songs which actually use backward extensions will be introduced in Book 2.

Although there is no expectation that the forward extension would be introduced at the Book 1 level, the songs which will eventually be used to introduce this skill are listed at the back as an available reference.

Shifting. The option of starting in third position provides an early opportunity to demystify the higher positions and avoid students becoming overly attached to a single position. The following additional options are available:

- *The Clocks* can be played in its original key of D / G major, but with *mi* on first finger (second position). The high *do* is a perfect opportunity to shift to the high harmonic. This can be introduced whenever the teacher wishes to offer an interesting, novel and accessible shifting experience.
- *Naughty Kitty* can be played starting in second position; this is appropriate for a later Book 1 student.
- *Shady Grove* offers an easy and satisfying shift to fourth position, with the highest note falling on a ring tone (C).

Shifting and position work will not play a mandatory role in students' repertoire until Book 2.

Scales & Bowing Patterns. Scales and bowing patterns are introduced near the beginning of students' study, and follow a parallel development alongside students' Book 1 repertoire journey.

Developing bowing patterns and skills well before these arise in the literature increases students' awareness of bow usage and overall finesse, as well as providing an opportunity for the patterns to feel comfortable and fluid by the time the skill eventually does appear.

Meanwhile, the patterns provide interest, challenge, and varied repetition for each new scale which is introduced, both during this book and in the later books.

Song Checklist. The song checklist at the back of this book provides a helpful organizational tool for the teacher, as well as a concrete way for students and parents to visualize their progress.

I hope you enjoy using this book, and I look forward to meeting and collaborating with you!

Please reach me at elise@discoverviolin.org anytime with your edits, thoughts, suggestions, and student stories. I would love to hear from you.

Elise

Listening daily is the key to confident progress and excellent musicality.

discoverviolin.org/
book1-cello-audio

◀ Listen to the audio recording twice daily, playing in the background as your family goes through the day. This will provide a model for the cello sound and help with internalizing the solfège (do, re, mi) words of the songs.

Watch and listen to Annie Jacobs-Perkins performing the Book 1 songs, absorbing her posture and bowing, as well as the nuances of how the songs are played. ▶

discoverviolin.org/
book1-cello-video

Key to Symbols

ⓓ The letters *d*, *r*, *m* etc. refer to *do*, *re*, *mi*, etc. in movable-do solfège. The larger the circle, the longer the note value.

⟲ means "circle bow" (a counter-clockwise lift through the air, when playing with the bow).

:‖ means repeat the song or section.

⊓ means "out-bow."

V means "in-bow."

♩ A dot above or below a note means *staccato* (stopped bowstrokes, with pauses in between).

"Do clef" is used in movable-do solfège to indicate the tonality of a piece without the use of sharps and flats. The base of the "d" circles the tonic note, which can be assigned to any pitch. This allows a song to be executed in any key without changing the notation. "Do clef" is a standard Kodály notation convention.

"So clef" is used for the Mixolydian song *Old Joe Clark*.

"La clef" is used for the Aeolian *Shady Grove*.

"Re clef" is used for the Dorian song *Crabfish*. The three non-standard clefs are used to help novice players orient the notes of the modal melodies around the tonic as little effort as possible.

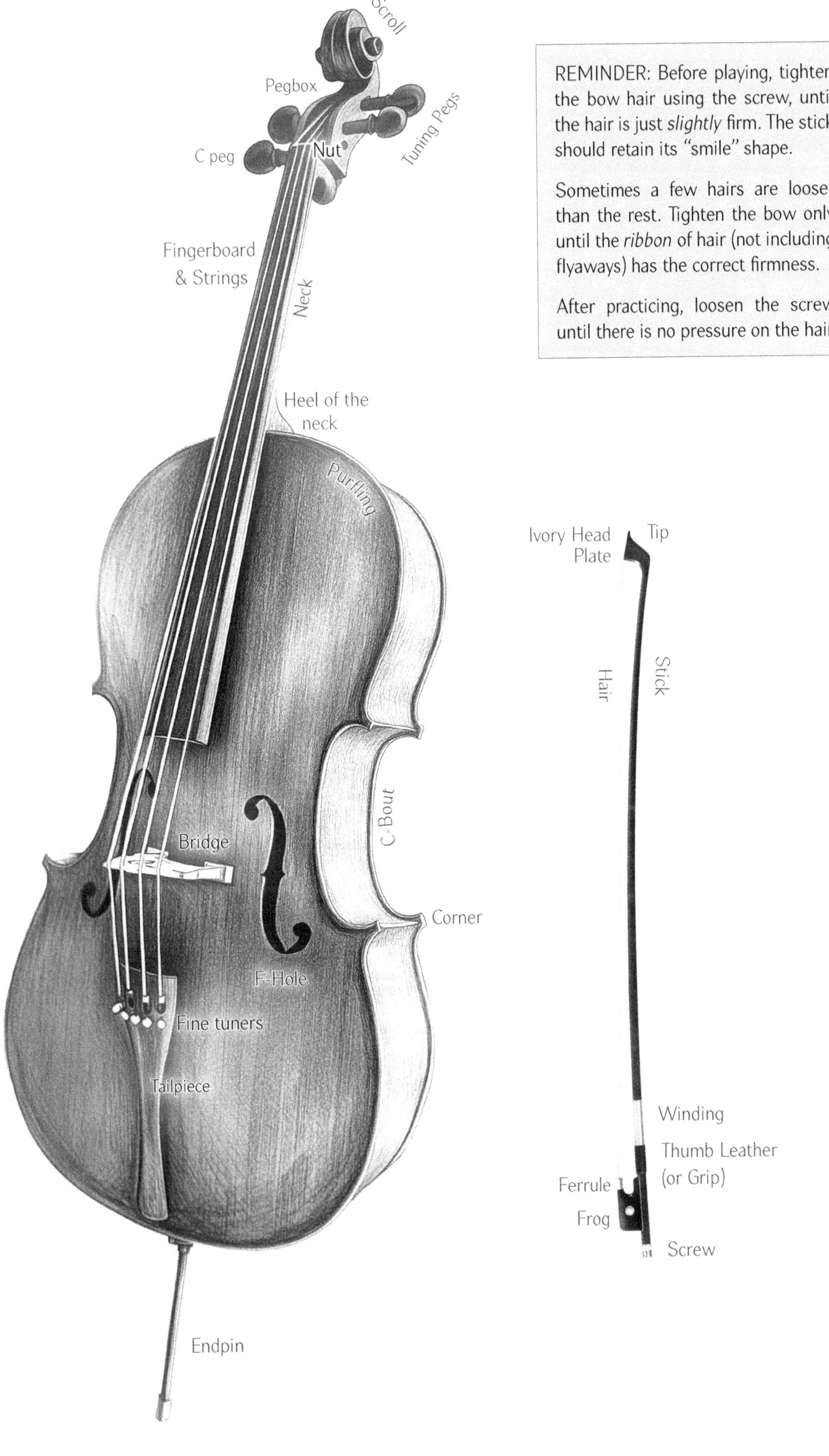

REMINDER: Before playing, tighten the bow hair using the screw, until the hair is just *slightly* firm. The stick should retain its "smile" shape.

Sometimes a few hairs are looser than the rest. Tighten the bow only until the *ribbon* of hair (not including flyaways) has the correct firmness.

After practicing, loosen the screw until there is no pressure on the hair.

Setting the Cello Posture

Setting the Cello & Endpin

First, select a chair which is the correct height and is firm and stable. Avoid seats that slope inward or are heavily cushioned. A cello chair or cello stool is ideal; these can be adjusted frequently as the student grows.

Adjust the seat so that the hips are slightly higher than the knees. The feet should be under the knees, with toes pointing slightly outward in line with the knees.

The three contact points of the cello are as follows:

- The heel of the cello neck rests lightly on the chest, just left of the sternum, over the heart.
- The left knee fits into the curve just below the C bout.
- The C peg brushes the nape of the neck, or falls just behind the left ear.

Each student's body is proportioned a bit differently, so individual contact points vary slightly. During the lesson, once the teacher has established your ideal individual setup, take a photo so you can easily recreate this posture at home.

Finding Your Playing Position

- Sit on the front half of the chair. This allows for the downard slope of the legs.
- The cello should be at approximately a 45° angle to the ground.
- The cello should face forward, with a very slight angle to the right from the player's perspective.
- The back should be tall and relaxed, with a very slight forward lean.*
- The left knee should gently support the cello. The right knee should be relaxed.

Hand and Arm Position

- The left arm should align with the back of the hand. The elbow lifts to access the lower strings.
- The left thumb rests lightly under the neck, across from the middle (second) finger.
- The thumb and middle finger form a "C" shape.
- The pinky should be perpendicular to the fingerboard, contacting the fingerboard on its tip.**
- The first finger will be angled as necessary. It may be bent, and will likely contact the string on the side of the finger rather than the tip.
- Both shoulders should remain relaxed when the arms are raised during bowing and fingering.

Bow and Bowhold

- The thumb is placed on the back of the bow just past the frog, on the back of the stick. It should be relaxed and slightly bent.
- The middle two fingers are across from the thumb, and drape over the frog.
- The bow is drawn at a right angle to the strings, with the bow hair parallel to the floor.
- The arm is relaxed, allowing the weight of the bow (rather than exertion) to create the tone.

* This counterbalances the cello and provides greater ease and reach for the bow arm.

** Parents and students may notice professional players' hands angled in various ways while vibrating and/or playing in higher positions. The starting position above serves as students' foundational setup.

NOTE FOR PARENTS

Your child should learn the songs in this collection through by-ear learning. This is accomplished by listening daily to the recording and singing along as often as possible.

Your child should be able to fluently sing each song in solfége before trying it on piano. This should happen naturally after a few weeks of listening and singing along.

Be sure not to have the book open while playing on piano or cello; instead, sing the song a few times with your child to rekindle the memory. All songs are played on piano in the key of D Major.

The pictorial notation in this book is intended as a visualization tool. Singing the song while pointing to the pictorial notation is a good tool for kinesthetic learning, especially for very young children. Following the notes in tempo is harder than you might expect! Your child will begin to experience melodic contour as they trace the rising and falling shape of each melody.

If your child loses the thread of the melody midway through a song, you can sing the next phrase for them as a reminder. You can also invite them to sing out loud as they play.

Quaker, Quaker

English

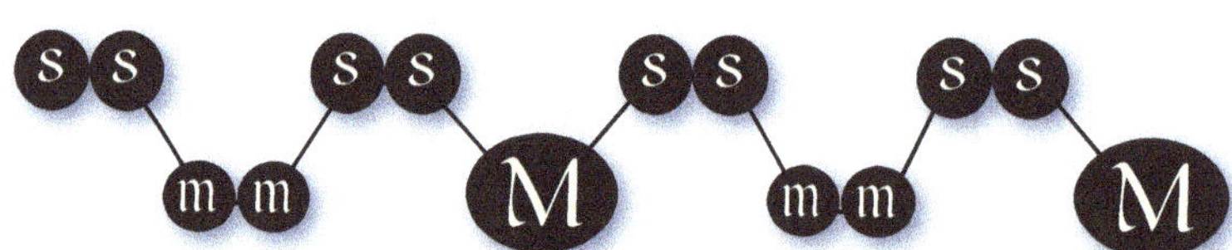

"Quaker, Quaker, how art thee?"
"Very well. I thank thee."
"How's they neighbor, next to thee?"
"I don't know, but I'll go see."

Pease Porridge Hot

English

Pease porridge hot, pease porridge cold,
Pease porridge in the pot, nine days old.

Some like it hot, some like it cold,
Some like it in the pot, nine days old.

Fireflies

by Elise Winters | Dorian

Fireflies appear at dusk
With luminescent lullaby
Flick'ring candles on their back
A quiet music in the sky.

Fireflies appear at dusk
As lanterns on a quiet pond
Flick'ring candles on their back
A sparkling nighttime sarabande.

Hot Cross Buns

English

Hot cross buns,
Hot cross buns.
One a penny, two a penny,
Hot cross buns.

Boil Them Cabbage Down

American

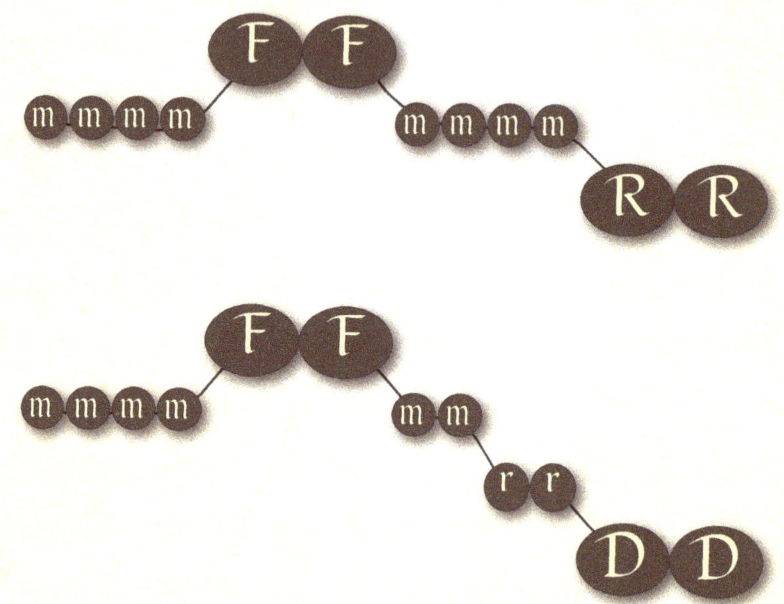

Boil them cabbage down, down,
Bake them hoecakes brown, brown,
The only song that I can sing
Is "Boil Them Cabbage Down."

Possum in a 'simmon tree,
Raccoon on the ground,
Raccoon says, "You son of a gun,
Shake some 'simmons down!"

How to Make Hoecakes

Hoecakes are a traditional Southern breakfast food. They got their name because they were originally cooked over a fire outdoors, on a garden hoe.

1 ¼ cups water
1 cup finely ground white cornmeal
1 teaspoon sugar
½ teaspoon salt
Butter (or bacon fat)
Honey (for serving)

1. Combine the cornmeal, sugar, and salt in a large glass bowl.
2. Heat the water to a rolling boil.
3. Add the boiling water a little at a time, stirring constantly. Continue adding water until the mixture is smooth and thick enough to plop off the spoon in a blob. *The boiling water helps pre-cook the cornmeal in the bowl.*
4. Heat a skillet or griddle to medium high. You'll know it's hot enough when you flick a drop of water on the pan and it skitters across the surface.
5. Grease the skillet well with butter or bacon fat.
6. Drop the batter by the tablespoonful onto the skillet.
7. Lightly tap each puddle of batter in several places with the edge of your spatula to release any air.
8. Leave each hoecake in its place until the edges begin to brown, 5–6 minutes.
9. Once this happens, flip and keep frying until the cake is cooked through, 4–6 minutes longer.
10. Serve these hoecakes to your family with butter and honey while they are still hot! Meanwhile, finish making the rest, adding more grease to the skillet as needed.

Let Us Chase the Squirrel

American

Let us chase the squirrel,
Up the hickory, down the hick'ry,
Let us chase the squirrel,
Up the hick'ry tree.

If you want to catch him,
Up a hick'ry, down a hick'ry,
If you want to catch him,
Climb you up that tree.

All My Little Ducklings

German

Alle meine Entchen
Schwimmen auf dem See,
Schwimmen auf dem See,
Köpfchen in das Wasser,
Schwänzchen in die Höh'.

All my little ducklings
Swimming in the sea,
Swimming in the sea,
Heads are underwater,
Tails look up at me.

All my little goslings
Gather by the pond,
Gather by the pond,
Roaming through the grasses,
Mama looking on.

The Clocks
"Store Ure Siger," Danish RoundW
M M
d d dddd D D
s s s s
m m mmmm m m m m
d'd'd'd' d'd'd'd' d'd'd'd' D
s s ssss
Grandfather clock says
tick-tock tick-tock
Cuckoo clock says,
tick-a-tock-a, tick-a-tock-a,
Pocket clock says,
tickaticka tickaticka tickaticka tick!
EXCELLENCE IN PUNCTUALITY
White Rabbit

All Around the Buttercup

English

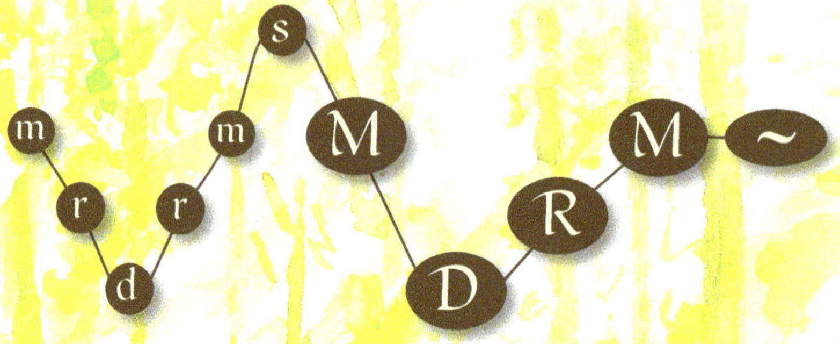

m r d r m s M D R M ~

m r d r m s M M R D ~

All around the buttercup,
One, two, three,
If you want a bonny lass,
Just choose me.

All around the clover white,
One, two, three,
If you want a bonny lad,
Just choose me.

Mary Had a Little Lamb

English

Mary had a little lamb,
Little lamb, little lamb,
Mary had a little lamb whose
Fleece was white as snow.

Everywhere that Mary went,
Mary went, Mary went,
Everywhere that Mary went
The lamb was sure to go.

Poor Little Kitty

English

Poor little kitty puss,
Poor little feller,
Poor little kitty puss,
Down in the cellar.

Twinkle, Twinkle

"Ah! vous dirai-je, Maman," French | English

Ah! vous dirai-je, Maman,
Ce qui cause mon tourment
Papa veut que je retienne
Des verbes la longue antienne
Moi, je dis que les bonbons
valent mieux que les leçons.

Twinkle, twinkle, little star
How I wonder what you are
Up above the world so high
Like a diamond in the sky,
Twinkle, twinkle, little star
How I wonder what you are.

Naughty Kitty Cat

English

Naughty kitty cat!
You are very fat.
You have butter on your whiskers,
Naughty kitty cat.

Naughty kitty cat!
You are very fat.
You have liver on your whiskers,
Naughty kitty cat. SCAT!

NOTE TO PARENTS: A few solfège words are provided below to help students transition to note-reading. While it may seem helpful to write the remaining solfège, we suggest instead helping your child practice understanding the visual pattern of steps and skips, while learning the song by ear using the recording.

There's a Hole in the Bucket

American

s, l, d r d

There's a hole in the bucket, dear Liza, dear Liza,
There's a hole in the bucket, dear Liza, a hole.

Well, mend it, dear Henry, dear Henry, dear Henry
Well, mend it, dear Henry, dear Henry, mend it!

Button, You May Wander

English

Button, you may wander, wander, wander,
Button you may wander ev'rywhere.
Bright eyes will find you, sharp eyes will find you,
Button you may wander ev'rywhere.

Toddy-O

American

Pass one window, Toddy-O,
Pass two windows, Toddy-O,
Pass three windows, Toddy-O,
Jingle at the window, Toddy-O.

Toddy-O! Toddy-O!
Jingle at the window, Toddy-O.
Toddy-O! Toddy-O!
Jingle at the window, Toddy-O.

Hush-a-Bye

"Arrorró" | Mexican

Arrorró, mi niño, arrorró mi sol,
Arrorró, pedazo de mi corazón.
Este niño lindo no quiere dormir
Y el pícaro sueño no quiere venir.

Hushabye, my darling,
Hushabye, my soul,
Darkness falling round you,
In your cradle warm.

Frère Jacques

French

Frere Jacques, Frere Jacques,
Dormez-vous? Dormez-vous?
Sonnez les matines, sonnez les matines,
Din din don, din din don.

Are you sleeping, are you sleeping
Brother John, Brother John?
Morning bells are ringing, morning bells are ringing
Ding ding dong, ding ding dong.

This Old Man

American

This old man, he played one,
He played knick-knack on my thumb,
With a knick-knack, paddywhack, give a dog a bone,
This old man came rolling home.

Two ... shoe
Three ... knee
Four ... door
Five ... hive
Six ... sticks
Seven ... heaven
Eight ... gate
Nine ... spine
Ten ... once again

Butterfly and Kangaroo

"Borboletinha" | Brazilian

Translation by Elise Winters

Borboletinha tá na cozinha
Fazendo chocolate para a madrinha
Poti poti perna-de-pau, Olho de
vidro e nariz da pica-pau pau pau!

The butterfly is in the cupboard
To make a chocolate cake for her godmother
A cup of cocoa, a bit of glue,
A melted crayon and a kangaroo, roo, roo!

The butterfly is at the station
To take a train to her vacation
She put the cake upon the rack, and
instead of butterflying, she butter-sat, sat, sat!

The kangaroo was quite perturbed
To find herself caught up in the strange dessert
She left that train at Sao Luis
And gave away the cake to her kanga-niece,
niece, niece!

Old Joe Clark

American | D Mixolydian

Old Joe Clark, he had a house;
Fifteen stories high
And every story in that house
Was filled with chicken pie

Fare thee well, Old Joe Clark
Fare thee well, I'm bound
Fare thee well, Old Joe Clark
Goodbye Betsy Brown.

The Koi

"Poissons de la Mélancolie," French

French text by Guillaume Apollinaire, adapted | Translation by Elise Winters

Dans vos viviers, tapies dans vos étangs,
Comme, ô carpes, vous vivez longtemps!
Est-ce la mort qui, rêvant, vous oublie,
Défiant le temps et glissant vers la nuit?
Poissons amis de la mélancolie.

Marigold fish in the deep of the pond,
Time passes by, yet you somehow swim on,
Humans, we all must grow old and decline,
You seem to slip past the mortal design,
Swimming through water and swimming through time.

Bingo Was His Name

American

There was a farmer had a dog,
And Bingo was his name-O,
B-I-N-G-O ....
And Bingo was his name-O.

There was a farmer had a dog,
And Bingo was his name-O,
[clap]-I-N-G-O ...
And Bingo was his name-O.

There was a farmer had a dog,
And Bingo was his name-O,
[clap] [clap] -N-G-O ...
And Bingo was his name-O.

Continue removing one letter per verse until the third line is simply the clapped version of the rhythm.

Love Somebody

Appalachian

Love somebody, yes I do
Love somebody, yes I do
Love somebody, yes I do
Love somebody but I won't tell who.

I'm my mama's darling child
I'm my mama's darling child
I'm my mama's darling child
I ain't gonna marry for a good long while.

Yankee Doodle

American

Yankee Doodle went to town
Riding on a pony
Stuck a feather in his hat and
Called it macaroni.

Yankee Doodle keep it up,
Yankee Doodle dandy,
Mind the music and the step,
And with the girls be handy.

Father and I went down to camp,
Along with Captain Gooding,
And there we saw the men and boys
As thick as hasty pudding.

32

Shady Grove

American | D Aeolian*

* Technically the key of Shady Grove is la pentatonic, since there is no sixth scale degree (fa); however, Aeolian provides a more familiar modal reference.

Shady Grove, my little love
Shady Grove I say
Shady Grove, my little love
I'm bound to go away.

Cheeks as red a blooming rose
And eyes are the prettiest brown
She's the darling of my heart
Sweetest girl in town.

The Birds' Wedding

"Ein Vogelhochzeit," German

Translation by Elise Winters

Ein vogel wollte Hochzeit machen in dem grünen Walde,
Fidi ra la la, fidi ra la la, fidi ra la la la la la.

Sonja Sparrow wants to marry in the greenwood forest ...
Baron Bunting is the bridegroom, with his cape fine woven ...
Aldegunda, noble owl, has gathered all the creatures round ...
Linnet with his minstrels gay will sing for them a merry lay ...
Hildebrand the Grand Peacock will dance for them a fine gavotte ...
Gretel Quail and Gunther Grouse will build for them a treetop house ...

The Crabfish

American | D Dorian

"Fisherman, fisherman, standing by the sea,
Hast thou a little crabfish tha'st could sell to me?"
Mash a row dow dow dow diddle all the day,
Mash a row dow dow dow diddle all the day.

He took the fish home, his wife was asleep,
And he put him in the sink alive to keep ...

To wash her face in the night she rose
And the crabfish grabbed her by the nose! ....

"Oh help! dear husband; come take a look!"
And the crabfish both their noses took ....

The Cabbage Patch

Book 1
Skills & Checklists

Introductory Activities

Songs on the Piano (D Major)

First learn each hand separately. When ready, play both hands together ("copy-hands").

- [ ] PREQUEL: Giraffes and Elephants

- [ ] Pease Porridge Hot
- [ ] Hot Cross Buns
- [ ] Let Us Chase the Squirrel
- [ ] Boil Them Cabbage
- [ ] All My Little Ducklings
- [ ] Mary Had a Little Lamb
- [ ] Naughty Kitty Cat
- [ ] Twinkle, Twinkle
- [ ] Button, You May Wander
- [ ] Frere Jacques
- [ ] Poor Little Kitty

Cello Movement Building Blocks

These building blocks are designed as practice activities during the early stages of learning the instrument, with the motions being to the beat of the corresponding song.

Most of the building blocks are done without the cello. 𝒞 and 𝔅 denote exercises which use the cello and/or bow.

A third-position hand placement is used for comfort and visibility. The finger locations do not matter; the focus is shaping the hand and arm.

- [ ] Let Us Chase the Squirrel. ***Tree Dives.***

1. Begin with the thumb on the left shoulder in a large "C" shape.
2. Touch the left knee with the fingers of the left hand, allowing the hand to open.

- [ ] Love Somebody. ***Body & Head Angle.***

Verse 1: Sit upright in the chair, with the feet centered. Lean forward slightly; this is playing position. Stand up. Then return to the leaning position. Repeat this sequence.

Verse 2: Move the hand from the knee to playing position (near the shoulder). Simultaneously glance at the hand using just the eyes (don't turn the head). Return both hand and eyes to their starting position.

- [ ] Bingo. ***Ball Squeezes.*** Use a rubber ball a bit smaller than the child's hand for the following activities:

Verse 1: Squeeze the ball with all the fingers of the left hand.

Verse 2: Squeeze the ball with just the three pinky-side fingers.

- [ ] All My Little Ducklings ***Bird Wings.*** From standing position, hold the arms out with palms facing the floor. Bring the thumbs into the sternum. Raise and release the elbows.

- [ ] Hush-a-bye. 𝒞. ***The Cello Hug.***

1. Sit with the cello using correct posture.
2. Gently drape the arms around the shoulders of the instrument, resting the hands loosely over the fingerboard with the right hand on top.
3. Rock side to side, moving the spine and pelvis together as a unit.

- [ ] Butterfly and Kangaroo. ***Clinging Fingers.*** Curve the fingers of both hands, and hook them together, with the left hand on top. Pull them in opposite directions while keeping them hooked together. Try wiggling your thumbs!

- [ ] Button You May Wander 𝒞. ***Tall Body, Hanging Arm.***

1. Establish the cello posture. Test the stability of the trunk by the parent gently pushing inward on the left arm, and inward on the sternum. Test the stability of the left knee by gently pushing outward.
2. The student rests their bow hand in the palm of the parent's hand, releasing the weight fully.
3. The parent moves the arm around, making sure the arm remains limp throughout the song.
4. Did the body remain tall and stable while the arm "wandered"?
5. Now do the same thing with the student making slow, relaxed circles with the bow arm, like a water wheel.

- [ ] Old Joe Clark. ***Banjo Pinky.*** Sing the song while plucking the G string of the cello using the pinky of the left hand.

- [ ] Buttercup 𝔅. ***Bear in the Meadow.*** Form a bowhold on the bow. Begin with the bow in vertical position.

First phrase: Do a "stir the pot" motion. The bear is running around the meadow.

Second phrase ("one-two-three"): Loop the left thumb into the tip of the bow, and pivot the bow into a horizontal position. Raise the frog while keeping the tip still. This is like pivoting to the A string. The bear has climbed the hill to see across the valley.

Repeat this sequence for the third and fourth phrases of the song.

Boil Them Cabbage ℬ. *Ride the Rails.*

1. Grasp the bow stick a few inches from the tip with the left hand. Hold it at waist level.
2. Drape the right-hand fingers loosely over the stick, approximately on the middle joint.
3. Slide the bowhold up and down the bow, maintaining the same contact points.

This Old Man *Banana & Scissors.*

Peel the Banana: Hold the left hand with the palm facing down and all the fingers touching. Practice opening the pinky from the rest of the hand; then the index; then both simultaneously.

Scissors: Again make a flat palm. Open the fingers with two on each side.

1. Open & close pinky
2. Open & close index
3. Peel the Banana
4. Scissors

Quaker, Quaker. *Thumb Doorbell.*

1. Place the right thumb against the middle finger, just below its first fold. The thumb should be slightly bent.
2. Lay the left-hand fingers under the bow fingers for support.
3. Use the left thumb to press and release the bow thumb., "ringing the doorbell" of the thumb.

Birds' Wedding 𝒞. *Bouncing Fingers.*

Verses 1-4: Place one finger on each cello string, approximately in second position (no tapes are needed). The pinky will be on the highest string, perpendcular to the string. The index will be on the lowest string, lying slightly on its side. The hand and arm should be aligned.

Press one finger for each verse, with all the fingers remaining on their respective strings. The pressing finger remains resting on the string when the pressure is released.

Verse 5: Place all the fingers on the G string and press simultaneously.

Verse 6: Place all the fingers on the C string. Press the fingers as a group, *four times*. Then do the same thing on G, D, and A.

The arm should transport the fingers to each string, with hand and arm staying aligned and the wrist straight.

Later, when the student is ready, press the string just twice (going up the strings then back down again).

Yankee Doodle *Captain & Soldiers.*

Verse: Touch the tips of left-hand fingers 2-3-4 to the thumb. The index finger alternates pointing up and closing into a compact square shape.

Refrain: The first finger stays standing tall, while fingers 2-3-4 alternately stand and curve, with the fingertips touching the thumb.

Paw Paw Patch 𝒞. *First Finger Independence.*

1. Place all the left-hand fingers on the G string, approximately in second position.
2. Bend and open the first finger of the left hand, keeping the other fingers resting on the string, and the thumb released.

Twinkle, Twinkle. *Moonflowers.*

Close the left-hand fingers to the palm with the thumb closed on the side.

3. Point up the 1st, 2nd, 3rd, then 4th finger slowly like a flower opening or a paper fan, stretching the first finger slightly back as it opens.
4. Close them in the reverse order.

Each opening and closing is four beats of the song.

Hole in the Bucket 𝒞ℬ. *String Tugs.*

1. Make a bowhold and place the bow on the G string of the cello. Drape the left hand loosely over the strings.
2. Using the relaxed weight of the arm and a bit of lean into the index of the bow hand, sink into the string and tug it back and forth, without making a note.
3. Move to a different string for each verse of the song, using the micro-beat of the song.

The Clock. *Broomstick.*

1. Hold a 1" wooden dowel in front of the body, near waist level, by grasping it with the index and thumb of both hands. Both palms should be at approximately a 45° angle to the ground.
2. Slide the hands outward, allowing the elbows to "wing" upward.
3. Now slide them inward until the "finger rings" meet again, making sure both elbows release downward.

Crabfish. *Swishing the Water.*

1. Pretend you have just added more hot water to a bathtub of water. Swish your right hand horizontally through the water to mix it in. The wrist should lead in both directions, and the palm should be at approximately a 45° angle to the ground.
2. When ready, do the same thing with a pencil bowhold, keeping the pencil on a straight path.

The Koi. ℬ. ***Seaweed Pinky.***

1. Place a chopstick or pencil between the bow stick and hair. Hold it near waist level, parallel with the floor.
2. Make a bowhold on the bow.
3. Draw the bow left and right, allowing the hand to pivot. The pinky curve will release as the bow reaches the tip. The pinky tip should maintain contact with the bow.

The center of the pivoting motion is the tip of the thumb, and the tip of the middle or ring finger on the ferrule.

If the pinky needs more stability, a "pinky house" can be made out of a corn cushion, cut in half and fastened to the frog with the straight edge at the top of the bow stick.

Shady Grove. ***See Saw, Rowing, & Log Rolls.***

Make a bowhold on a pencil, with the point facing left.

1. ***See Saw***. Manipulate the fingers to pivot the pencil lik a see saw.
2. ***Rowing***. Unfold and re-curve the fingers, moving th pencil away from you and back.
3. ***Log Rolls***. Manipulate the fingers to trace a circle wit the point, pivoting around the thumb and middle finge This establishes a stable pivot point around the thum and middle finger.

Bow Hand & Bow Awareness

This section focuses on the balance of the arm, momentum, planes of movement, and the "feel" of the bow stick.

The objective and instructions for these exercises and those on the next page can be found in *The Balanced Violinist*. The page numbers are indicated next to the exercise title.

Angles & Movement

Deep Sea Dive 64

Rowing 65

Criss-Cross:

1 Balance point 2 Middle 3 Tip

Puddle Jumps & Rainbows 66

1 Middle to frog

2 Middle to tip

3 All 3 positions

✓ Bow circles. Alternate between two-handed bow circles (grasping the tip with the right hand) and traditional bow circles with just the bow hand.

G & D strings A & C strings

Bow & Arrow

Cheese Nibbles & Cheese 67

TECHNIQUE TRAINING

Graduation of patterns marked with a ★ may be honored with a special sticker placed on the front cover, or another desirable incentive.

Practice each rhythm on 1) open strings and 2) scales. Master the basic version of a variety of exercises before adding advanced versions within each set. As new keys are learned, mix and match patterns and keys.

BOWING PATTERNS

v Huckleberry 70-71
- [ ] Echoes
- [ ] 4-note scale on G / D
- [ ] Huckleberry, Huckleberry
- [ ] Huckleberry, Huckleberry with bear hug

- [ ] Chocolate Ice Cream 70

v Popcorn Ball ("Out-Out, In-In") Hooked bows 71
- [ ] 4-note scale
- [ ] Feathered endings
- [ ] ★ Popcorn Ball & Popcorn

v Peanut Butter Cracker 71
- [ ] Open strings, 4x per string
- [ ] 4-note scale
- [ ] ★ With metronome, ♪=104
- [ ] Tonic triad, ____ Major 74

v Raisin Bread 72
- [ ] Silver wrap bowhold
- [ ] Frog bowhold
- [ ] Upside-Down Raisin Bread

v Bread and Cheese 72
- [ ] Out-bow
- [ ] In-bow
- [ ] ★ Advanced
- [ ] With metronome, ♪=74

v Bow & Arrow 66
- [ ] ⊓ on G & D strings
- [ ] ⊓ On A string
- [ ] V on all strings

v Gooseberry 72
- [ ] Gooseberry Pie
- [ ] V Gooseberry Pie
- [ ] ★ Gooseberry, Gooseberry
- [ ] Gingersnap, Gingersnap
- [ ] ★ Gooseberry Pie with metronome, ♩=60
- [ ] Tonic triad, ____ Major 74

- [ ] Woodpecker 73

v Kiwi 74
- [ ] Out-bow
- [ ] In-bow

v Waffles for Breakfast 74
- [ ] On piano, with metronome, ♪=93
- [ ] On cello
- [ ] ★ With metronome, ♪=110

- [ ] Slur Exercise 74

METRONOME

Accommodate the tempo to the student's ability, using the suggestion as a loose starting point.

Hot Cross Buns (♩=70):	[ ] Listen: Is it together?	[ ] Sing	[ ] Play on Piano	[ ] Play on Cello
Boil Them Cabbage (♩=63):	[ ] Listen: Is it together?	[ ] Sing	[ ] Play on Piano	[ ] Play on Cello

Mini Practice Breaks

The activities below are perfect to use as a break during practice. They refresh the attention, build strength and coordination, and rekindle joyfulness and connection.

Move

Bear Walk. Walk on all fours across the room and back.

Crab Crawl. Walk on all fours, tummy upward. This builds shoulder and abdominal strength.

Kangaroo Hop. Cross the room using large jumps with both feet.

One-Legged Goose. Hop across the room on just one foot.

Wheelbarrow. Walk the hands while the parent holds the legs. This builds shoulder & arm strength.

Sidestep. Step sideways, then feet together. Finish with a side jump!

Heel to Toe. Walk forward heel-to-toe along a line. Then do it backwards!

Half Grapevine. Walk sideways by crossing right foot over left. Cross left over right to go the other way!

Full Grapevine. Again cross right over left, but alternate crossing in front and in back. Now reverse it!

Bounce

Ball Bounce. Find a room with a large area that is safe for throwing. Use bounces to pass the ball.

Ball Toss. As above, but passed through the air. Optional: Back up one step after each successful pair of passes.

Stretch

Lava Flow. From a standing position, gradually bend at the waist until your fingers brush the floor. Place each hand on the opposite elbow and continue sinking even lower. Swing your arms side to side. Then return to standing, unfurling slowly, with the head returning last.

Squeeze the Grapefruit. Squeeze together the shoulder blades toward the center of the back.

Shoulder Shrugs. Lift shoulders to ears. Hold, then release.

Triceps Stretch. Place both arms above the head, forming a box, with each hand on the opposite elbow. Pull one arm toward the opposite side, then the other.

Balance

Balance activities are both stimulating and calming.

Toe Painting. Balance on one foot, then use the other to draw shapes in the air. Spell your name, or draw a picture.

Telescope. Extend the arms with hands clasped together, pointing the index fingers. Use the whole upper body as a telescope to point to items on the ceiling, walls, and floor.

Balance Beam. Make a balance beam by elevating a length of 4x4 fencepost on two blocks. Practice stepping, walking heel to toe, standing on tiptoe, turning, etc.

Release

Whirligig. Spin your torso side to side, leading with your nose. Make your arms like spaghetti noodles, so they whip side to side. Allow the heel opposite the twist to release slightly from the ground.

Jumping Bean. Parent and child hold hands together and jump up and down 20 times.

Rag Doll. The parent moves each arm all around, gently but unpredictably. Occasionally let it drop. Was it loose as a rag?

SONGS PROGRESS CHART

Song			
Quaker, Quaker smsms	3rd pos	1st pos	
Pease Porridge Hot SmmS	3rd pos	1st pos	
Fireflies rmfltlfm	3rd pos	1st pos	
Hot Cross Buns MRD	G	C	
Boil Them Cabbage Down mmmmFF	G	C	
Let Us Chase the Squirrel ddrrMS	G	C	☐ Alternate bow directions ☐ String crossings: keep bow on string
All My Little Ducklings drmfSS	G	C	☐ Staccato and legato notes
The Clocks DDdddd	1st pos	2nd pos	
All Around the Buttercup mrdrmsS	D	C	
Mary Had a Little Lamb mrdrmmM	D	C	☐ Smooth and connected
Poor Little Kitty RrdmrD	D	☐ Bow division	

 Learn at home with parent's help

 Bonus assignment for this week

 Keep working on it

 Almost! Play it perfectly (no mistakes) the first time.

 (Foil star) Congratulations! This is now a review song. Review many songs each practice to make them better and easier!

 Review specifically assigned by teacher

Twinkle, Twinkle ddslIS	D	C	☐ Feathered phrase endings
Naughty Kitty Cat sslIS	D	C	☐ All notes staccato ☐ Start in 2nd position
Hole in the Bucket drMDS,	D	C	☐ Legato string crossing
Button, You May Wander dddrMS	D		☐ Smooth & connected ☐ Pause bow slightly for silent 4th finger hops
Toddy-O msslmsS	D	C	☐ Silent string levels, no fingers ☐ Silent string levels, add fingers
Hush-a-Bye mrfmDD	D		☐ ♩=80 ☐ Add slurs on *so-la* and *mi-re*
Frere Jacques drmd	D		☐ ♪=80 ☐ ♪=96 ☐ ♪=112
This Old Man smSsmS	D	C	☐ LONG "ta" notes ☐ All staccato except ♬ notes
Butterfly and Kangaroo s,L,S,dd	C		
Old Joe Clark rmfmrdT,	D Mix. 1st pos.		
The Koi D'D'D'	D	C	
Bingo s,dds,s,lls,	C		
Love Somebody dmssrmF	C		
Yankee Doodle ddrmdmr	C		

Shady Grove LLtlS	D Aeolian 1st pos.	
The Birds' Wedding smsmfrfr	C	
The Crabfish lLLr'r'r'r'	D Dorian	

Backward Extension Songs

Key of E♭ Major or second position F Major, except as noted

- [ ] Hot Cross Buns
- [ ] Buttercup
- [ ] Mary Had a Little Lamb
- [ ] Twinkle (1st position F Major)
- [ ] Poor Little Kitty
- [ ] Toddy-O (first two phrases)
- [ ] Butterfly and Kangaroo (1st position E♭ Major)

Forward Extension Songs

Key of E♭ Major or second position F Major, except as noted. This is considered a Book 2 skill, but the songs are listed here as an available reference.

- [ ] Pease Porridge Hot
- [ ] Squirrel
- [ ] Ducklings
- [ ] Clocks (low A major)
- [ ] Frere Jacques
- [ ] Button

www.ingramcontent.com/pod-product-compliance
Lightning Source LLC
Chambersburg PA
CBHW041134120626
46547CB00019B/2992

9781959675082